This book belongs

Find me hiding on every page!

Copyright © 2024 Mary Ransom
All rights reserved

A Big Future
For A Little Shark

Mary Ransom

"Hello, my name is, Little Shark,
I live in the open sea."

"I know I'm small, but soon I'll grow,
I wonder what I'll be!"

"I could be a Mako,
Selling taco's from a van."

"I could be a Horn Shark,
Performing for my fans."

"Perhaps I am a Black Tip,
Who will learn to read and write."

"Or maybe I'm a Lantern Shark,
With a fairy light."

"I could be a Hammerhead,
Building sheds and wooden barns.

"I could be a Lemon Shark.
Picking fruit from a farm."

"Maybe I'm a Silk Shark,
A natural fashion queen."

"Or even a scary Ghost Shark,
Hunting on Halloween."

"I want to be a grown up,
Not just a Little Fish."

"To grow up big and strong,
That would be my wish."

"I could be a Megamouth,
Singing in a band."

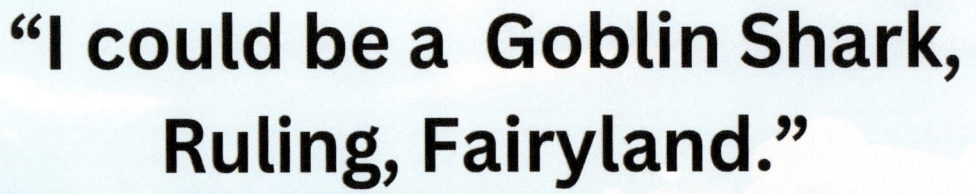

"I could be a Goblin Shark, Ruling, Fairyland."

"Perhaps I am a Nurse Shark,
Who will help sad fish to laugh."

"Or maybe I'm a Tiger Shark,
Hiding in the grass."

"I could be a Blue Shark,
Making blue vein cheese."

"I could be an Angel Shark,
Flying in the breeze."

"Maybe I'm a Bull Shark,
Made for giving rides."

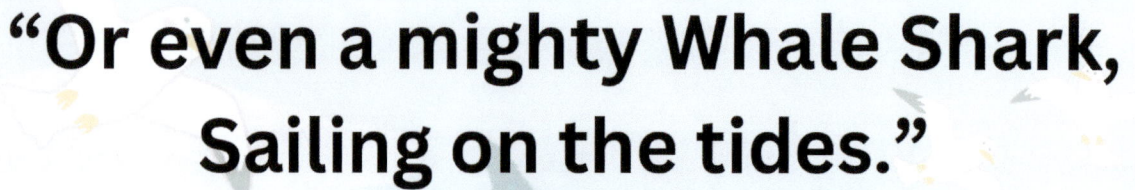

"Or even a mighty Whale Shark,
Sailing on the tides."

"I really don't know what to choose,
And guessing is so tough."

"I've got to find out what I am,
Before the seas get rough."

"I could be a Cookie Cutter,
Making treats for all my friends."

"I could be a Basking Shark,
Weaving brand new trends."

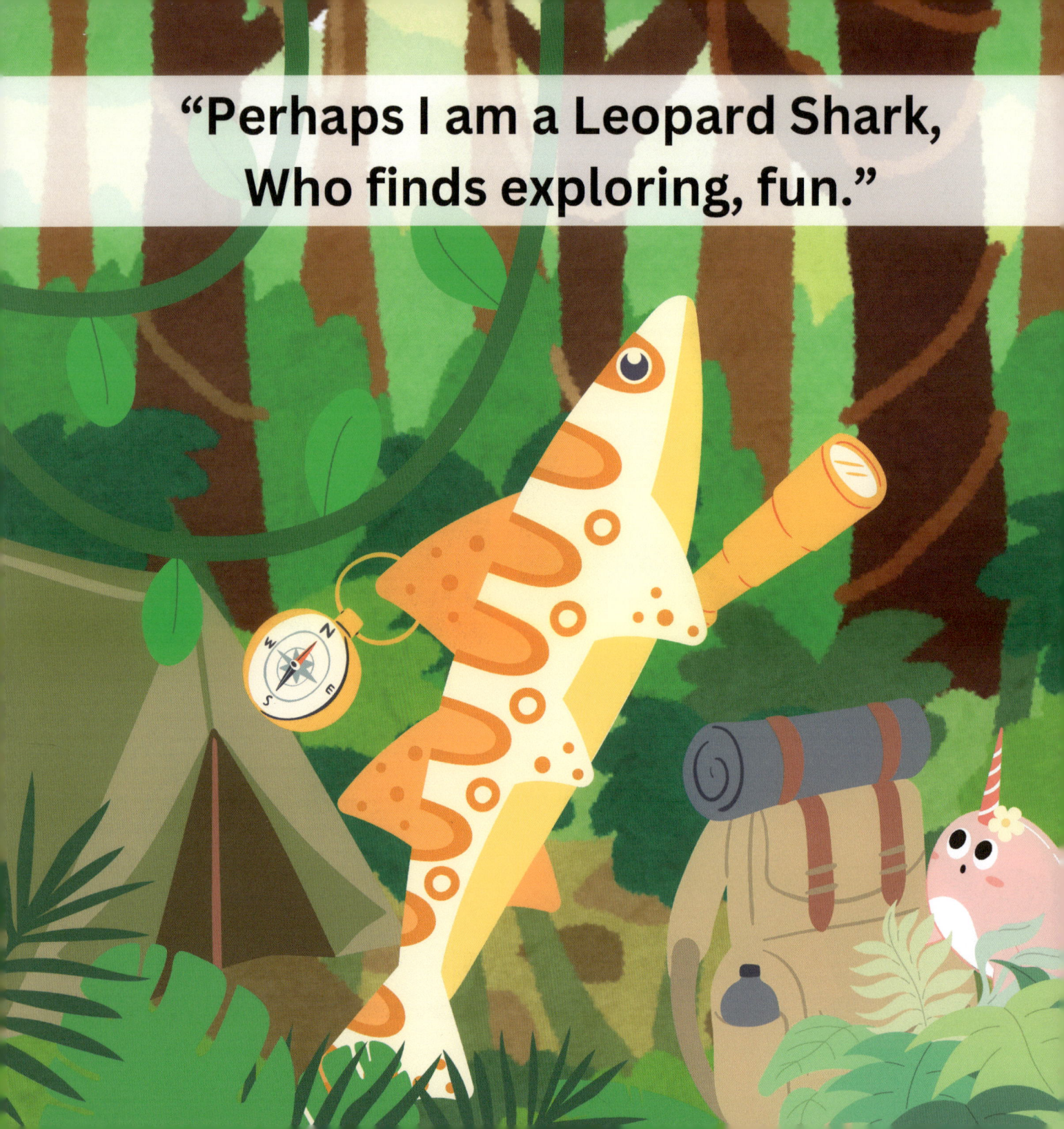

"Perhaps I am a Leopard Shark,
Who finds exploring, fun."

"Or maybe I'm a Zebra Shark,
Taking photo's in the sun."

"There's lots of things I want to know,
But now it's getting dark."

"Maybe tomorrow, I'll find out,
That I'm a Pacific Sleeper Shark."

Printed in Great Britain
by Amazon